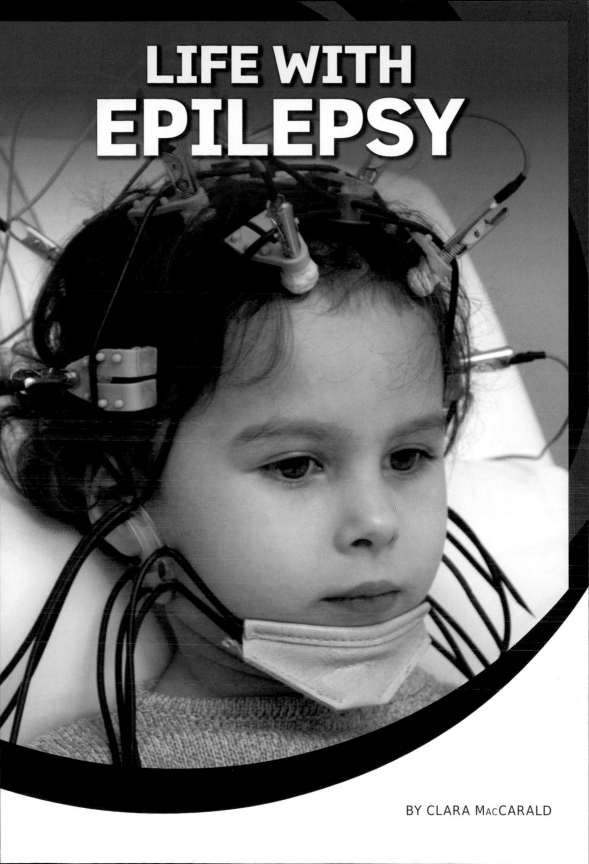

LIFE WITH EPILEPSY

BY CLARA MacCARALD

Published by The Child's World®
1980 Lookout Drive • Mankato, MN 56003-1705
800-599-READ • www.childsworld.com

Content Consultant: Jean Cibula, M.D., Professor and Division Chief for Epilepsy
at the University of Florida, Board Certified in Adult Neurology with a subspecialty
certification in Epilepsy and Clinical Neurophysiology

Photographs ©: BSIP/Universal Images Group/Getty Images, cover, 1; iStockphoto,
5, 20; Image Source/iStockphoto, 6; Xi Xin Xing/Shutterstock Images, 9; Shutterstock
Images, 10, 14, 16; Ted Pagel/Shutterstock Images, 12; Yakobchuk Viacheslav/
Shutterstock Images, 18

ISBN 9781503825116
LCCN 2017959679

Printed in the United States of America
PA02375

TABLE OF
CONTENTS

FAST FACTS

- **Epilepsy** is a condition that causes **seizures**.

- Seizures are the primary **symptom** of epilepsy. Our brains use electrical signals to communicate between cells. Seizures happen when this electricity gets out of control. People may freeze or shake during a seizure.

- You cannot catch epilepsy from someone else. Sometimes other health conditions, injuries, or problems in the brain cause epilepsy. Other times, the cause is unknown.

- Approximately 70 percent of people with epilepsy can stop their seizures using medicine. The other 30 percent still have seizures even though they take medicine. Sometimes a brain operation or the **keto diet** can help stop seizures.

- More than 65 million people around the world have epilepsy. Approximately three million of these people live in the United States.

- Seizures come in two main types: focal and generalized. **Focal seizures** act on only part of the brain. They might make only one part of the body move or freeze. **Generalized seizures** act on the whole brain.

SEIZURE TYPES

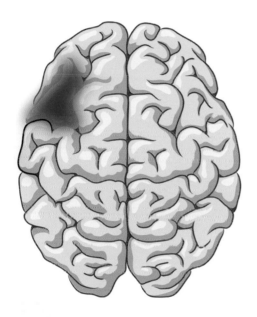

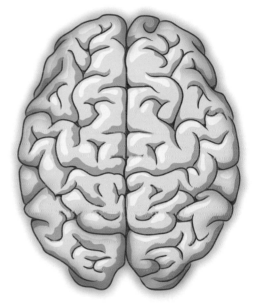

FOCAL
SEIZURE

GENERALIZED
SEIZURE

Chapter 1

A SURPRISE SEIZURE

One morning, eight-year-old Lily sat on the edge of the bathtub and watched her mom comb her sister's hair. Lily was happy to relax. The family was going through a hard time. They had been forced to move suddenly. She was starting at a new school.

Lily looked at her long hair in the mirror. Suddenly, Lily saw her own face begin to move strangely. She had no idea what was happening. Scared, but thinking fast, she waved at her mom while she still could. Her mom screamed. Her dad ran in, grabbed Lily, and brought her onto the bed in the bedroom.

◀ Epilepsy can happen to any person at any age. It is more common in younger and older people, however.

Her family looked on helplessly until Lily stopped shaking. They crowded around her. Like many people do after a seizure, Lily had trouble talking. She sat on the edge of the bed, scared about what just happened.

While her sister headed to school, Lily went to the doctor. The doctors didn't have answers at first. Sometimes people have one seizure without having epilepsy. The seizure had frightened Lily, but not knowing how to stop them worried her more.

WHAT TO DO

If someone is having a seizure, never hold them down or put anything in their mouth. If no adult is around, send someone to find one. Move objects out of the way and lay the person on their side if you can. Seizures look scary, but most people who have one will be fine. The person may be confused or tired afterward. Let them know they are safe.

Lily later went back to school. While playing on the playground, she had another seizure. Now the doctors knew Lily had epilepsy. They put her on medicine, which worked. She no longer had to fear seizures.

▲ **Going to the hospital can be scary sometimes, but doctors are there to help.**

Chapter 2

A FURRY CLASSMATE

Eight-year-old Dylan rolled out of bed on the first day of school. He felt nervous about the new year in a new classroom. Wanting to be prepared, he checked his bag after breakfast. He and his sister took first-day photos on the front step. Finally, he held his dog Elly's leash. Her red harness looked sharp against her smooth gold hair. They set off for school together.

Elly is not just a regular pet. She's also a **service dog**. Unlike people, some dogs can sense when a person is about to have a seizure. When Elly senses Dylan is in danger, she starts licking him or barking.

◄ Service dogs have to go to school just like kids. They are trained to help people.

Sometimes Dylan is afraid a seizure will hurt him. Elly helps give Dylan time to get help. After a seizure, Elly lays her head on Dylan's lap to help him be brave.

At the classroom door, the teacher welcomed Dylan and Elly. She took them to Dylan's desk, which had his name on it. Elly had a name tag, too, on a mat next to Dylan. She lay down as the other kids arrived.

Everyone crowded around to see the dog in the classroom. They knew not to touch her, though. Elly had a sign that said "Service Dog." The teacher told everyone to take their seats. Elly looked relaxed, but Dylan knew his best friend was watching him. Knowing he could have a seizure at any time was scary. Thanks to Elly, Dylan could pay attention to learning rather than to his epilepsy.

◄ Service dogs usually wear vests while they are working. This is so people know that they are helping someone and not just a pet.

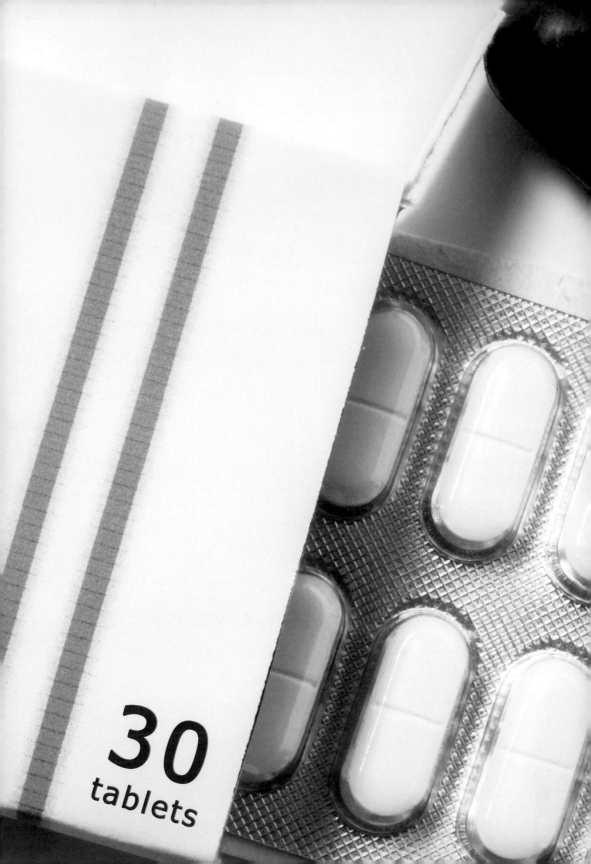

30
tablets

Chapter 3

EAT YOUR MEDICINE

Brian, a nine-year-old boy, hopped off the school bus. He flung his front door open. He yelled to his mom that he was hungry, and dropped his backpack on the floor.

Instead of telling him to hit the fridge, Brian's mom headed for a computer in the kitchen. She started planning his snack. Brian was on a special diet to help control his epilepsy.

Like some people with his condition, Brian used to have many seizures. They would happen even though he took medicine. In the middle of doing something like talking or climbing, Brian's body would suddenly freeze.

◄ **Medicine is the most common way to help reduce seizures for people with epilepsy.**

▲ **When following the keto diet, it's important to eat high fats, such as nuts, eggs, and avocados.**

After several seconds, his body would unfreeze. Sometimes people with these kinds of seizures make small movements or their bodies bend forward. To Brian, life used to be like watching a movie skip.

Thanks to the keto diet, his seizures stopped.

Although he was hungry, Brian sat at the table and waited. His mom weighed slices of meat, an apple, and a handful of nuts. Brian would have loved to eat a cookie, but to do so could cause the seizures to return.

Finally, his mom set Brian's snack in front of him. He gobbled it down. He made sure to eat every piece. After thanking his mom, Brian ran back out the door, ready to play. Although he didn't always like eating a special diet, Brian loved living without the pauses.

KINDS OF SEIZURES

Some people know before a seizure hits. They may hear strange sounds or see weird shapes. Other people have seizures without warning. Seizures can even happen when people are sleeping. Seizures come in many different types. Some cause a person's body to make lots of unusual movements. During other types of seizures, a person moves very little or not at all.

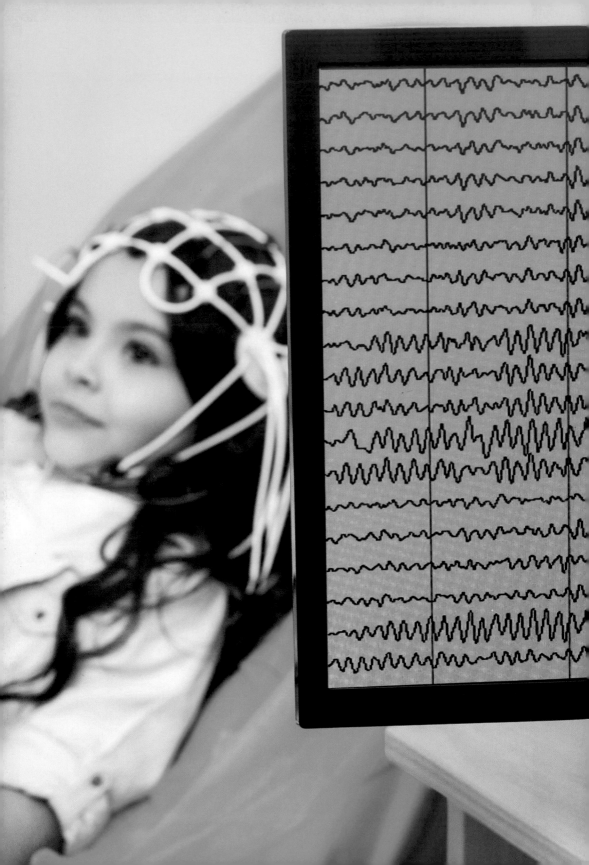

Chapter 4

SPYING ON BRAIN WAVES

Nine-year-old Emma staggered out her door into the cool morning air. She hadn't slept at all the night before, following her doctor's orders. She had struggled to keep her eyes open. Even movies lost their appeal as the night dragged on. Now Emma climbed into her mom's car to go to the hospital. She was about to have her first **EEG**, a test often done on people with epilepsy.

Emma and her mom walked down the long hallway of the hospital. Doctors welcomed them into a special lab room. They asked Emma to sit on a hospital bed. Her mom assured her the test wouldn't use needles. She kept very still. She was curious and a little nervous.

◀ **Doctors monitor a computer screen during an EEG test. The screen shows the person's brain wave pattern.**

▲ In order to measure brain activity, doctors will place between 16 and 25 electrodes directly onto a person's head.

A doctor began to glue **electrodes** to Emma's head. Each electrode had a little white patch over it. The electrodes would record electrical pulses in Emma's brain. A person with epilepsy may have unusual brain wave patterns, especially after not sleeping.

Tired after her long night, Emma fell asleep. After a few hours, the doctors let her go home for more sleep.

The doctors would use the test results to learn about the type of epilepsy she had.

Emma continued to go to the doctor as she got older. Unfortunately, Emma still had seizures sometimes. But she learned how to live with them, and with EEGs. Even though she didn't always like going to the doctor, she knew the EEGs helped keep her safe.

THINK ABOUT IT

- If you had to eat a special diet to stop seizures, would you do it? What if you still had some seizures, but fewer than before?
- Most people with epilepsy have no warning before a seizure. How might that change their life?
- Do you think having a dog in the classroom would make it easier or harder for someone with epilepsy to learn? What about other students?
- Think about people who live with different medical issues than you. How do you think you can help or support them?

GLOSSARY

EEG: An EEG is a test that looks at a person's brain waves. Doctors often use EEG results to learn about a person's epilepsy.

electrodes (i-LEK-trodes): Electrodes are points that let electric currents flow in or out of a machine. The EEG test uses electrodes to look at electricity in a person's brain.

epilepsy (EP-uh-lep-see): Epilepsy is a condition that causes people to have seizures. People with epilepsy take medicine to control their condition.

focal seizures (FOH-kuhl SEE-zhurz): Focal seizures are sudden attacks that act on only part of the brain. An EEG might find out if a person has focal seizures.

generalized seizures (JEN-ur-uh-lyzd SEE-zhurz): Generalized seizures are sudden attacks that act on all of the brain. Some people with epilepsy have generalized seizures.

keto diet (KEE-toh DYE-it): The keto diet is a special high-fat diet that helps some people with epilepsy. Brian had no seizures while he was on the keto diet.

seizure (SEE-zhur): A seizure is a sudden attack that happens when electric signals go out of control in a person's brain. Dylan's dog lets him know when he is about to have a seizure.

service dog (SUR-viss DOG): A service dog is a dog trained to help people with health conditions. People shouldn't pet a service dog because the animal is busy doing its work.

symptom (SIMP-tuhm): A symptom is a sign of an illness. Seizures are a symptom of epilepsy.

TO LEARN MORE

Books

Ballard, Carol. *How Your Brain Works.* New York, NY: Gareth Stevens, 2011.

Bender, Lionel. *Explaining Epilepsy.* Mankato, MN: Smart Apple Media, 2010.

Laughlin, Kara L. *Seizure-Alert Dogs.* Mankato, MN: The Child's World, 2015.

Web Sites

Visit our Web site for links about epilepsy:

childsworld.com/links

Note to Parents, Teachers, and Librarians: We routinely verify our Web links to make sure they are safe and active sites. So encourage your readers to check them out!

SELECTED BIBLIOGRAPHY

"CPL Seizure Alert Dogs." Canine Partners for Life. *Canine Partners for Life,* n.d. Web. 4 Dec. 2017.

Devinsky, Orrin. *Epilepsy: Patient and Family Guide, Third Edition.* New York, NY: Demos Medical Publishing, 2008. Print.

"What is Epilepsy." Epilepsy Foundation. *Epilepsy Foundation,* n.d. Web. 4 Dec. 2017.

INDEX

ABOUT THE AUTHOR

Clara MacCarald is a freelance writer with a master's degree in biology. She lives with her family in an off-grid house nestled in the forests of central New York. When not parenting her daughter, she spends her time writing nonfiction books for kids.